What do you call a baby
    scorpion? : and other baby
Author: Nathan, Emma.
Reading Level: 4.4
Point Value: 0.5
ACCELERATED READER QUIZ# 40812

471158

595.713
NAT

Nathan, Emma.

What do you call a
baby scorpion? : and
other baby spiders
and insects

431284 01595   56135B   001

What Do You Call a Baby Scorpion?

And Other Baby Spiders and Insects

EMMA NATHAN

BLACKBIRCH PRESS, INC.

WOODBRIDGE, CONNECTICUT

Published by Blackbirch Press, Inc.
260 Amity Road
Woodbridge, CT 06525
web site: http://www.blackbirch.com
e-mail: staff@blackbirch.com

© 1999 Blackbirch Press, Inc.
First Edition

Printed in Singapore

10 9 8 7 6 5 4 3 2 1

Photo Credits
Cover: ©Ed Ross; title page: ©Photodisc; page 3: ©Photodisc; pages 4, 6, 8,
13, 14, 19, 22: ©Ed Ross; page 5: ©Scott Camazine/Photo Researchers; pages
7, 8 (silhouette), 9, 10, 11, 12, 15, 17, 21: ©Corel Corporation; page 16: ©Patti
Murray/Animals Animals; page 18: ©Garry Watson/Science Photo Library;
page 20: ©E.R. Degginger/Animals Animals.

Library of Congress Cataloging-in-Publication Data
Nathan, Emma.
    What do you call a baby scorpion? : and other baby spiders and
insects / Emma Nathan.—1st. ed.
          p. cm.—(What do you call a baby—)
    Includes bibliographical references. (p.   )
    Summary: Provides the special names for such baby insects and
arachnids as the grub, maggot, and spiderling, describing their physical
characteristics and behavior.
    ISBN 1-56711-361-3
    1. Insects—Infancy—Juvenile literature. 2. Arachnida—Infancy—
Juvenile literature. [1. Insects 2. Arachnids. 3. Animals—Infancy.] I. Title. II.
Series: Nathan, Emma. What do you call a baby—
QL467.2.N28 1999   99-20242
595.713'9—dc21   CIP
                                    AC

Contents

What do you call a baby scorpion?

3

◆◆WHAT DO YOU KNOW?◆◆

Baby, You're an Instar

Scorpions may look like insects, but they're not. They are arachnids, like their relatives, spiders and mites. Arachnids have eight legs instead of six (which is the leg count for all insects). Arachnids also don't have compound eyes or antennae. Many baby insects, however, are also called instars, just like scorpions!

What do you call a baby ant?

Ants at a Glance

In an ant nest the queen runs the show. She is often more than three times the size of the worker ants in her colony. The queen is also the one who gives birth to all the antlings, which average 500 per brood!

What do you call a baby beetle ?

••WHAT DO YOU KNOW?••

Grub-A-Dub-Dub

Baby beetles are the most common baby animals on earth! If you count sheer numbers, there are more beetles in the world than any other animal. Some grubs, like the white grub of the June beetle, like to eat a lot. They really like eating the roots of grasses and other plants and can do serious damage to your lawn!

What do you call a baby butterfly?

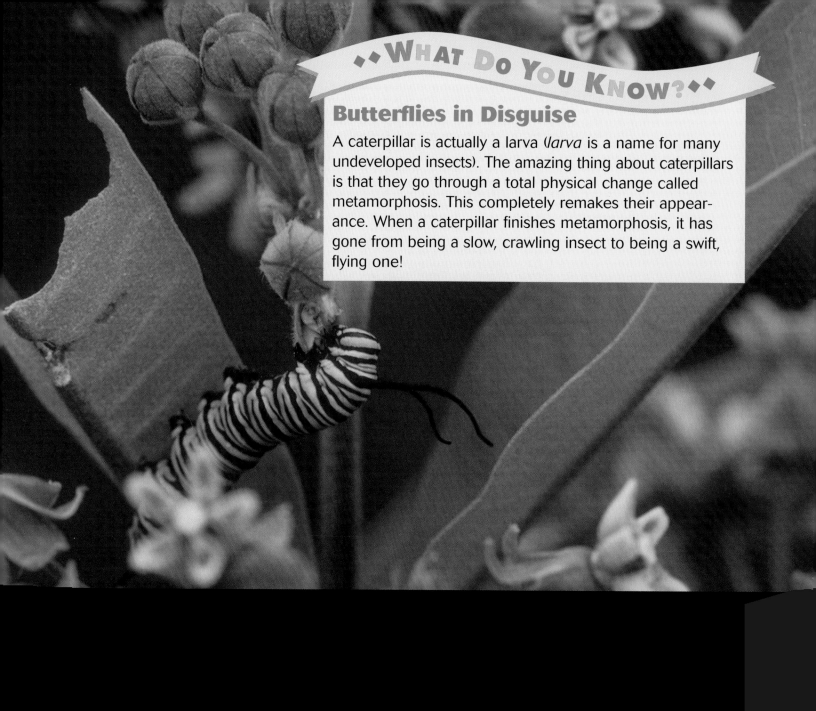

Butterflies in Disguise

A caterpillar is actually a larva (*larva* is a name for many undeveloped insects). The amazing thing about caterpillars is that they go through a total physical change called metamorphosis. This completely remakes their appearance. When a caterpillar finishes metamorphosis, it has gone from being a slow, crawling insect to being a swift, flying one!

What do you call a baby firefly?

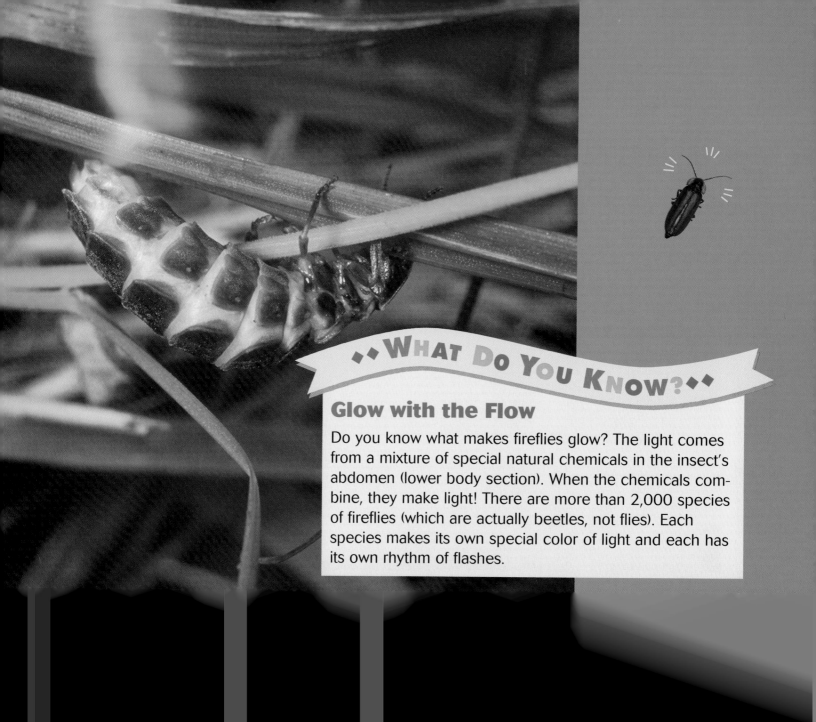

Glow with the Flow

Do you know what makes fireflies glow? The light comes from a mixture of special natural chemicals in the insect's abdomen (lower body section). When the chemicals combine, they make light! There are more than 2,000 species of fireflies (which are actually beetles, not flies). Each species makes its own special color of light and each has its own rhythm of flashes.

What do you call a baby antlion?

13

Oodles of Doodles

Adult antlions look a lot like dragonflies. But baby antlions look very different. As larvae (developing insects) they have huge appetites and attack other insects fearlessly. They especially like dining on ants! Many antlions live in sandy areas, where they dig shallow pits and wait inside for insects to fall in. Antlion larvae are called doo-dlebugs because, when they dig their pits, they make spiral-shaped trails in the sand. These trails look like "doodles."

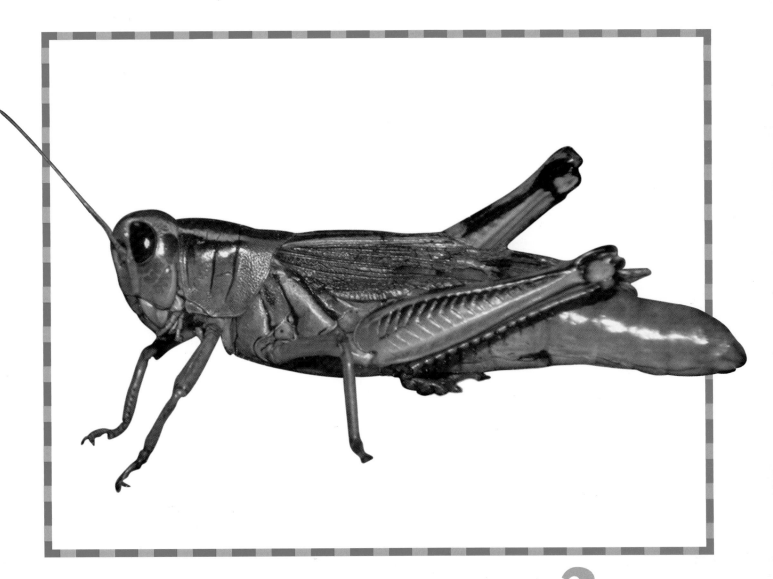

What do you call a baby grasshopper?

15

❖❖ WHAT DO YOU KNOW? ❖❖

A Hop, Skip, and a Jump

Like their insect relatives—dragonflies, termites, and cock-roaches—grasshoppers go through three stages in their life cycle. The first stage is as an egg. After they hatch, they are called nymphs. As nymphs, they look a lot like adults but they are much smaller. They also lack certain important body parts, such as wings. The final stage is the adult stage.

What do you call a baby fly?

Eggs, But No Legs

After hatching from eggs, legless maggots spend all their time eating and growing. As they grow, they shed their skin. When they are big enough, they pupate (wrap themselves up) and go through metamorphosis (complete physical change). Then, out of the pupa comes a fully developed adult fly!

What do you call a baby louse?

19

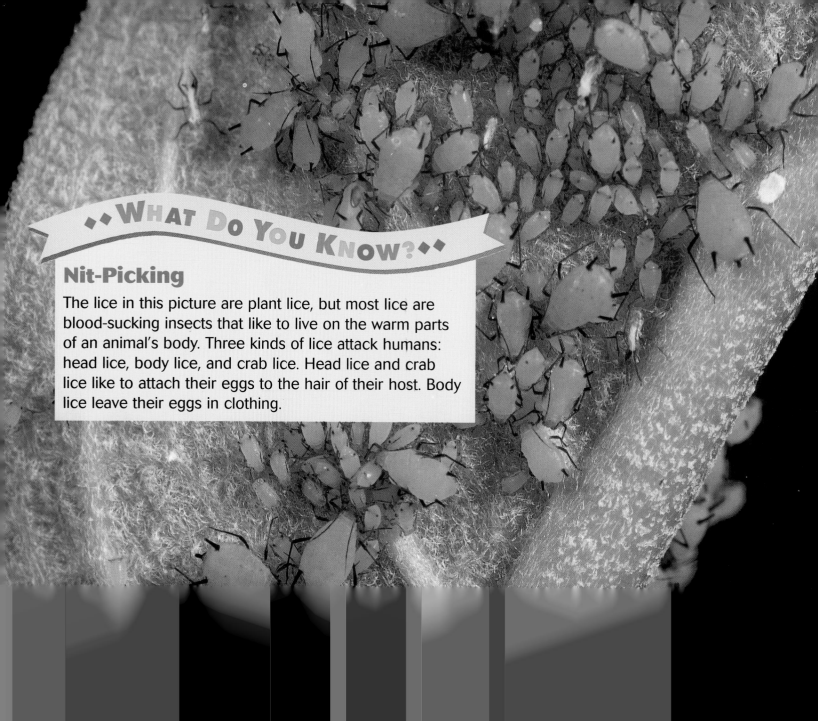

Nit-Picking

The lice in this picture are plant lice, but most lice are blood-sucking insects that like to live on the warm parts of an animal's body. Three kinds of lice attack humans: head lice, body lice, and crab lice. Head lice and crab lice like to attach their eggs to the hair of their host. Body lice leave their eggs in clothing.

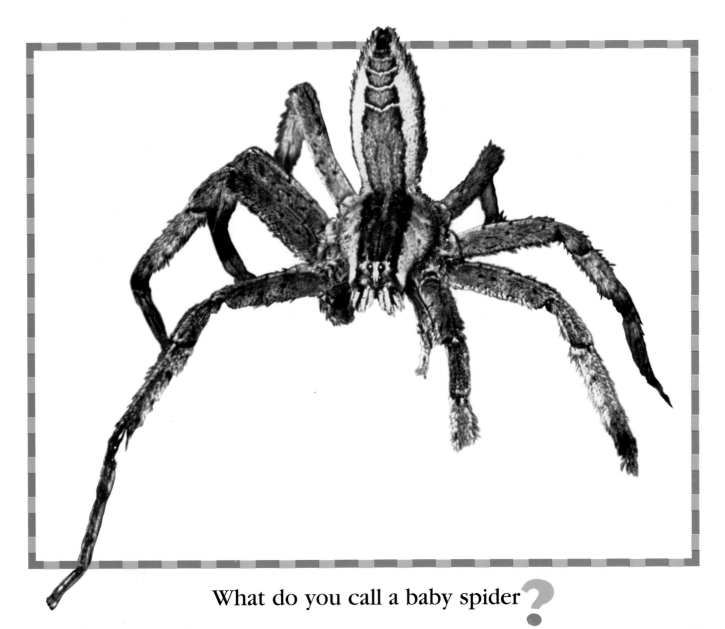

What do you call a baby spider?

21

Silken Spider Hider

An average-size spider will lay about 200 eggs at once. Larger tropical spiders, however, can lay up to 2,000 eggs at one time! Most females weave a silk sac (called a cocoon) around their eggs to protect them. Each spider egg contains a yolk, which nourishes the spiderling until after it is born.

Some Other Baby Insects and Spiders

Nymph	Larva	Caterpillar	Instar
grasshopper	*ant*	*butterfly*	*scorpion*
mosquito	bee	moth	molting mayfly
cockroach	gnat		molting silverfish
termite	hornet		
plant bug	wasp		
sand fly	silkworm		
	lacewig		

Glossary

Abdomen—the back section of an insect's body.

Antennae—feelers on the head of an insect that act as movable sensory organs.

Arachnid—an eight-legged animal with no antennae that has a body divided into two parts. Spiders and scorpions are arachnids.

Brood—a family of insects or animals.

Chemicals—substances that scientists study because their composition and properties can be changed.

Cocoon—a covering made from sticky threads produced by some animals to protect themselves and their eggs.

Colony—A large group of insects that live and work together.

Compound eye—an eye made up of many different lenses.

Larva—insect at the stage of development between an egg and a pupa when it looks like a worm.

Metamorphosis—the series of changes some animals go through as they develop from egg to adult.

Pupa—an insect at the stage of development between a larva and an adult.

Pupate—to become a pupa.

Species—one of the groups into which animals that share many characteristics are divided.

Yolk—the nourishing part of an egg. If the egg is fertilized, the protein and fat from the egg nourish the developing embryo.

For More Information

Books

Hunt, Joni Phelps. *Insects: All About Ants, Aphids, Bees, Fleas, Termites, Toebiters, & A Beetle or Two.* Morristown, NJ: Silver Burdett Press, 1995.

Koch, Maryjo. *Dragonfly Beetle Butterfly Bee.* New York, NY: Smithmark Publishers, 1998.

Pringle, Laurence. Gary A. Polis (Photographer). *Scorpion Man: Exploring the World of Scorpions.* Old Tappan, NJ: Atheneum, 1994.

Videos

Bill Nye the Science Guy: Reptiles and Insects—Leapin' Lizards! (Disney).

Web Sites

Antlion Pit: A Doodlebug Anthology
Behavior, life cycle, zoology, and observation of the antlion—www.enteract.com/~mswanson/antlionpit/welcome.html

Scorpion du jour
Scorpion terminology, identification, classification, photography, and information—wrbu.si.edu/www/stockwell/du_jour/scorpion_du_jour.html

The Butterfly Website
Features butterfly gardening, farming, observation, and conservation—www.butterflywebsite.com

The Wonderful World of Insects
Everything you ever wanted to know about thousands of insects—www.insect-world.com/main/six.html

Index